READING POWER

Transportation Through the Ages

Trains of the Past

Mark Beyer

10822132089

The Rosen Publishing Group's
PowerKids Press™
New York

Published in 2002 by The Rosen Publishing Group, Inc.
29 East 21st Street, New York, NY 10010

First Edition

Book Design: Christopher Logan

Photo Credits: Cover, p.13 (inset), 18–19 © Bettmann/Corbis; pp. 4–5 © Courtesy of The B&O Railroad Museum, Inc.; p. 6–7 © Underwood & Underwood/Corbis; p. 8–9 © Cumbres and Toltec Railroad/AP Wide World Photos; p. 9 (inset) © Jim Sugar photography/Corbis; pp.10–11, 14–15, 17 © Minnesota Historical Society/Corbis; pp. 12–13 © Milepost 92½/Corbis; p. 20 © Christopher Logan; p. 21 (top) © Bob Krist/Corbis; p. 21 (bottom) © David Samuel Robbins/Corbis

Beyer, Mark.
Trains of the past / by Mark Beyer.
     p. cm. – (Transportation through the ages)
Includes bibliographical references and index.
ISBN 0-8239-5986-4 (library binding)
1. Railroads–Trains–History–Juvenile literature. [1. Railroads–Trains–History.] I. Title.
TF550 .B49 2001
625.1'0973-dc21
                                                2001000653

Manufactured in the United States of America

Contents

Early Trains

The first trains in the United States were built in the 1820s.

Tracks

This train is from 1830. It had only one car. Horses pulled it on iron tracks.

Wheels

The *Atlantic* train was built in 1832. This train used a steam engine. It pulled two cars that carried people.

Steam Engine

The *Atlantic's* steam engine boiled water to make steam. The steam pushed bars up and down. The bars turned the wheels to make the train move.

Passenger Cars

Water Tank

By the 1860s, steam engines were big and powerful. They stopped to fill their big tanks with water. These trains pulled many cars.

The engineer drove the train. The fireman burned wood or coal to make steam.

Train tracks were built around the country. Railroad workers laid wood for tracks. Steel rails were put on top of the wood.

Wood Ties

Sometimes railroad workers had to break through rocks to lay tracks.

Some trains carried stone and coal. Stone helped build cities in the United States. Coal helped people heat their homes.

Stone and Coal

Some trains carried only people.
People rode trains to move from
one city to another.

Passengers

Riding on a Train

By the 1920s, train engines were twice as big as the old engines. They could pull ten cars and go 50 miles an hour.

Trains became the best way to travel. Families used them to travel all across the United States.

It was comfortable to travel on a train. People could eat on long trips. People ate while looking out the window.

Improving Trains

By the late 1940s, steam engines were replaced by diesel engines. Trains with diesel engines could go very fast.

These trains used diesel fuel. Diesel trains did not make the air dirty like the trains that burned wood or coal.

Some trains used electricity. Subway trains ran underground. They carried people to work.

People have been traveling on trains for more than 100 years.

Glossary

diesel fuel (**dee**-zuhl **fyoo**-uhl) a type of gas used to power train and truck engines

engineer (ehn-juh-**neer**) a person who drives a train

fireman (**fyr**-muhn) a person who put coal or wood into an oven that boiled water for steam engines

steam engine (**steem ehn**-juhn) an engine that used steam to move metal bars fixed to wheels

subway (**suhb**-way) an underground train that carries people

tracks (**traks**) iron or steel bars on which trains ride

Resources

Books

Ultimate Train
by Peter Herring
Dorling Kindersley Publishing (2000)

Trains of the Old West
by Brian Solomon
Barnes & Noble Books (1997)

Web Site
http://www.trains.com

Index

Word Count: 305

Note to Librarians, Teachers, and Parents

If reading is a challenge, Reading Power is a solution! Reading Power is perfect for readers who want high-interest subject matter at an accessible reading level. These fact-filled, photo-illustrated books are designed for readers who want straightforward vocabulary, engaging topics, and a manageable reading experience. With clear picture/text correspondence, leveled Reading Power books put the reader in charge. Now readers have the power to get the information they want and the skills they need in a user-friendly format.